Fran

Life is a poem
waiting to be written

Enjoy

Jerry Siegel

Sharing the Jerky

Poems to make you think, smile and celebrate life.

by
Jerry Siegel

Sharing the Jerky

Poems to make you think, smile and celebrate life.

Copyright © 2012 by Jerry Siegel

Copyright © 2012 by Cover design by Jacob Kubon

Cover Photograph by Jason Pratt

All rights reserved. No part of this book may be reproduced or transmitted in any form or by any means without written permission of the author.

Published by

splatteredinkpress.com

ISBN 978-1-939294-01-2

Dedicated to Mary Jo

ACKNOWLEDGEMENTS

In my first book I wrote of the things I learned about life while hiking on the Appalachian Trail. I shared how my love of the outdoors was developed as a child through experiences with friends and family while hunting and camping. Since then I have continued to hike, canoe, and reflect on life's purpose and meaning. Now I hike slower, smell the flowers more often, ponder and think about those previous outings while seeking learning and wisdom from those who are traveling life's journey with me.

It has occurred to me while observing the beauty of the wilderness, how many of the values and things I truly find important have become part of my life because of wonderfully strong women. I often find my thoughts and memories focusing on the truths and wisdom they have taught me, like sharing one's life with those in need.

Many of the ideas and words in this book I owe to my mother who always lived her life with dignity and kindness, putting her children and family first in everything. There is my beautiful and brilliant wife who is ever so patient, and shows genuine love, not only to our daughters and myself, but to all she meets. She has encourage me in so many ways, including putting my poems in book form to share with all who want to read them.

Thank you to my daughters. Jennifer, who not only read every poem that I have written but took the time to write a note of encouragement after reading each poem, and Becky who was a part of a lot of the camping experiences shared here.

I appreciate the many friends and family who have encouraged my writing and listened to my wandering thoughts over wine and cheese.

The title "Sharing The Jerky " comes from a hiker's gift of sharing a prized possession while on the trail. A hiker often freely volunteers to share the trail-mix as it is heavy to carry, but saves the lite jerky for one's self, reserving it for emergencies. I have learned the rewards and value of "sharing the jerky." I have had wonderful mentors who have taught me so much about love and kindness. If my poems have special meaning, these people deserve much of the credit.

Grab your pack and let's walk down the trail together, and let's share some jerky at our next trail break!

jerry (geraldpoet)

TABLE OF CONTENTS

PROLOGUE

INTRODUCTION
How to Read Poetry   4
Bad Poetry   5

IN THE WOODS
Sharing the Jerky   8
A Worm   10
Fall's Last Memories   11
First Moments of a New Day   12
Floating Orange Peels   13
Lilies   14
Snow   15
Snow at Searchmont   16
The First Snow   17

OUTDOOR LIFE
A Conversation With God   20
Afternoon Reflections
  on the Appalachian Trail   22
Backpacking in Life   23
Dreaming about the Appalachian Trail   24
Limping Into the Wilderness   26
My Greatest Poem Ever   27
Sitting By the Trail   28
We Are On The Trail   29
You Are Here   30

CAMPING

Campground Fly	32
Campground Mosquito	33
Campground Rain	34
In the Outback	35
Missanabi Stew	36
My Buddy's Wasted	37
My Old Tent	38
Old Refrigerator Food	39
Yummy Trail Food	40
Stirring the Pot	41

LOVE

Alaskan Ode	44
Expressions of Love	45
Love is Forever	46
My "Waiting for You" Song	47
Remember Me	48
To My Valentine	49
Whisper Your Name	51
Why I Write Poems	52
Why Give Your Love Flowers	53
It's Cold Here Tonight	55
Flowers	56
Happy Birthday	57
Love Lives Here	58
When You Were There	59

FAMILY

"Boy"	62
A Grandchild's Visit	63
Angie's Tree House	64
Cookie Prints	65
Family Reunion	66
Grandpa's Wilderness Camping Rules	68

I Need a Hug	69
My First Birdhouse	70
Grandpa Is The Best	71
Christmas Eve	72
Golf	73
Grandmother's Dishes	74
Jennifer	76
Rebecca	78
Cats	79
Losing Weight	80
Squirting the Stars	82
Shower Patina	83
The 90th Birthday	84
Valentine's Day	85

AGING

A Senior Moment With Technology	88
Athletes Beware	90
Beth's Golf Shack	92
Do Feet Get Enough Credit?	93
Good Neighbors	94
My First Pickle Ball Match	95
Now I Wander	97
Our Stories	98
Senior Bicycles	99
The Tip	100
They've Organized Old Age	101
Things are Getting Blurry	102
A Book	103
Condo Rules	104
I'm Gray & Still Working	105
Mr. Stiff-N-Achy	107
My Glasses	108
Old Men	109
Retired	110

First Day of School - Retired Teacher	111
The Best is Yet to Come	112

ON THE ROAD

A Canadian Sunrise	114
My Prayer	115
It's Raining in Prince Rupert	116
The Alaska I Remember	117
The Alaskan Way	118
The Brook	119
The City Camp	120
This River, Platte	121
Winter Prayer	122
Games Can Hear the Rain	123
Reflections on Two Beautiful Days In Goderich	124
New Car Meets the Trade-In	125
Reflections on a Paddle Down the Buffalo River in Arkansas	127
The Spirit of Beaver Isle	129
The Deer Hunters	130
Young Deer Hunter	131
Our Cars Interiors	132

REFLECTIONS

Little Lights	136
Me Climbing to Heaven	137
Morning Coffee	138
My Journal	139
Reflections on a School Year	140
The School Parking Lot	141
Willie's Last Day of School	142
The Things I Buy	143
This Moment is Mine	144
A Poem About You	145

I'm Running	146
It's Not About Me	147
Spiritual Walking	148
The Do It Now List	150
The Flavor of Words	151
The People That We Meet	152

PHILOSOPHY

Brothers	154
Choices Men Make	155
Different Opinions	156
life	157
Living in the Now	158
Our Place in the Universe	160
Owning Stuff	161
True Heroes	162
Why Do We Hate?	163
War	164

PROLOGUE

I started writing poetry to record beautiful moments and poignant observations for my own personal record of my life's journey. When sharing my writings I noticed that people often responded by looking more closely and more fully at their own life experiences and values. It is my hope you too may feel the need to "share the jerky" before you get to the end of the trail, and hopefully will find that even bad poems can stretch the mind and lift one's spirits.

INTRODUCTION

HOW TO READ POETRY

fishing is best done
with fishermen
Baseball best done
with a team
Thinking is best done
alone or
with engineers
Parties are more fun
with friends

But poetry is best written
alone
when beauty is all around
and best read by
candlelight
a glass of wine and
the beauty of your smile

together they make me feel like
Samuel Beckett or
William Shakespeare and
even Robert Frost

BAD POETRY

I like to write bad poetry
because
good poetry is hard to write
And
folks have such high expectations for it.

It's recited in
social circles of high regard
with such an air
by people who have pedigrees
and pompousness.

There are good things about words
poorly stated,
which don't rhyme
and look elementary.
It makes people feel superior,
they don't have to think too much,
they smile and grin when they read it,
no one worries about iambic pentameter
or whether its classic or new age.

Bad poetry lets me write about
dogs, trucks, trains, guns and bad behaviors.
I can use dangling participles and split Infinitives,
write thoughts and words common folk
understand and use to get through each and every day.

People of high society- blue bloods - would never
venture to use or read this type of poetry.

Bad poetry can be cool
on the street or even in school.
So the question for you is -
do you like bad poetry?
or just Browning,
Frost and
Homer?
Are you enjoying this?
This is a sad, bad poem……..
or maybe not ……….

IN THE WOODS

SHARING THE JERKY
(often the most important food to a hiker)

We share life's
leftovers, castoffs and
extra's,
food, books,
clothes that no longer fit
and even time
with the needy, poor and other
folks who aren't as
blessed as we

We sometimes even feel guilty
about money and
possessions we accumulate
don't use and often
really don't need

Cottages, second homes, and
sport cars left
unused most of the year
then
we buy weapons to protect our stuff

While some folks live in tents and walk out in the cold
we store extra money in the bank
we even green our lawns with
water while others die of thirst
But like the backpacker
heading down the trail
into the unknown
the heavy extra stuff -

apples, M&Ms©, cookies
are easy to share

Sharing our most valued possessions (jerky)
is oh so tough
Sharing leaves us
exposed and vulnerable
to a hungry world

And so we hold tight
to things we think
we will need

"This jerky is the best I have
the most important in my bag"
until the trail ends and
we see up ahead
or Hospice calls

Now we wished
we had shared
the jerky..........

A WORM

Who made
the worm
to slide
in the dirt
lie on
the driveway
after a rain?

I think
robins
had a lot to do
with making
worms

They seem
to eat them for
breakfast
lunch and
dinner
and sometimes
in between

But maybe
God made them.
I've heard she likes
to fish for trout

FALL'S LAST MEMORIES

trees drop
their golden leaves
one by one
soon to be naked
then lean inward
as if seeking to be hugged
for winter memories
of frost bite
and winter storms
are scars on
their bark

spring comes
far too slowly for these trees
who must shelter their
dormant buds
wishing the seasons could
change just a
little faster

FIRST MOMENTS OF A NEW DAY

Squinting through an eye lid crack
As thin as a dime
I see foggy light
Trying to see if this new day
Is grey or sunny bright

Already clothing questions
shorts, blue jeans or sweats
Invade my brain
 sounds of those alive,
 energizer bunny types
 begin to enter my awakening brain

Dogs barking, Cars starting,
distant garbage haulers
I wish for Just a few more minutes of
delightful slumber

I feel the results of yesterday's excesses
pains and aches from recent and distant past
I say a brief prayer for the new day
knowing it will keep me in
bed a few more minutes

What will I serve for dinner tonight
Is my slighted friend from yesterday
still angry with me?

My bladder, with a kick, ends
all procrastination
I smell brewing coffee
It's going to be a great day!

FLOATING ORANGE PEELS

it came
from Florida
once hung
in splendor
high up
in a tree

now
its floating
in a trout stream
its skin is turning brown
it smells
is wrinkled
and dry looking

its juice
and pulp
once tasted
so good

how it got here
I do not know
for oranges
aren't
a trout's first
breakfast choice

Worms or grasshoppers
suit them just fine

LILIES

Lilies and morning dew
go together
like snow and sleds
like tiny lights on Christmas trees.

People in love
go together
like frosting and cake
smiles and little babies.

But lilies and Easter
are like starting over
breathing fresh air
enjoying the first glorious morning
of spring.

SNOW

Little white crystals
fall and swirl
from the sky
into a dream world
where
fluffy white blankets
are
carefully being
laid over houses
cars
bird nests
and slow moving old men

SNOW AT SEARCHMONT

Drifting snow swirls
over hidden fences
the old barn is
slowly going under

Outside the window
snow is level with the sill
cars are mounds of
large marshmallows

Smoke curls from crevice like
miniature canyons
finding air so cold it
wants to return to log and fire
but dissipates in snowy air

This land gives charm
to city folk
who sit by the fire and
huff and puff about
traipsing in the snow

They eat and talk and
form their thoughts
about life in cabins
long ago.

THE FIRST SNOW

the still grey sky
trees everywhere without one leaf
no birds to sing
the grass a faded brown
lakes and ponds a frozen mass
a chilly wind from
the North blows
people scurry into
darkened buildings
to share the news
"It won't be long now!"

OUTDOOR LIFE

A CONVERSATION WITH GOD

The wind blows cold today
on the Appalachian Trail.
I eat oatmeal, drink my coffee,
and while lifting my pack I ask
"Please walk with me today God".

A friend would be nice today
in these strange woods with
mountains to climb.
What did you do yesterday God?
I hiked, rested and wrote a poem.

Did you visit India?
Do you know most Americans think You
live in the U.S. and just
visit other places?
Who would you visit if you weren't
with me today;
the president? famous people? a guy in prison?

Of all the places in the world,
why are you walking here with me?
Want to race to that big tree up ahead?
Tell me if I'm not being respectful enough.
Should I be dressed up to be talking with you?
When I eat jerky can you taste it too?
Why do I find you in the woods
more often than in church?
Have you ever talked to Socrates?

Was he as bright as folks think he was?

How is it that I know you are walking
with me and yet hear no footsteps?
Is it true that you spend more time
with those who read holy books?

This GORP is tasty,
God, want some?

AFTERNOON REFLECTIONS ON THE APPALACHIAN TRAIL

the sun is very warm
a cool breeze freshens the day from the shadows
this jerky tastes great
I sit beside the trail resting
the dogwood and azalea are spectacular
this mountain is high, damn high

buds and leaves are bursting
out of their winter clothes
into the warm sunshine
the sun begins to sink
behind a high mountain

I wonder where my hiking friends are ?
what are they doing ?
for years some have said
" I would love to hike the Appalachian Trail "
when asked ....
" I'm too busy, maybe next time "
I want to say, "This is next time "
time has quickly run out
there will not be a next time

I sit in this splendor alone
to fulfill a dream
it takes more than talk
for hikers you must walk the walk

my mind wanders back to a beautiful lady in Michigan
I pick a wild flower to remind me of her
it will be on my pillow tonight

BACKPACKING IN LIFE

I lift my pack
and wonder why
I need
all this heavy gear
is it the special things
I must have
to ease my time on
the trail
is it the extra things
to make the trip
less risky
is it the
things
that hold special memories
to remind me
of my past,
friends,
and life itself

I find the things
I take with me
weigh me down
make me tired
and
hold me back

Now my goal
for life
and on the trail
will be
to travel lite
climb
higher mountains
to see the world
as the
eagle does

DREAMING ABOUT THE APPALACHIAN TRAIL

As my head hits the pillow
I'm starting a trip down the trail
I feel my hiking stick in hand
my backpack heavy with food
my clothes are dry
my gear organized precisely
just right for this trip

I'm climbing
higher and higher
admiring the great views
suddenly the sky
is turning black
(does it rain in dreams)
I whip out my rain coat
put on my hat

Now its turning cold
I hike all day in the rain
there's even some sleet
but now
I'm in my tent
things are dry
my bag is warm
even my feet
I hear a large branch break
something falls on my sleeping bag
I jump up in bed

my cat
is on my chest
smiling at me

now it's time
to go to the bathroom
and when I return
to this very warm bed
I will dream
of a trip to the
MALL
LOWE'S
or HOME DEPOT
but not
a hiking trip in the mountains

LIMPING INTO THE WILDERNESS

I should have gone into the
wilderness years ago
in my prime
with defined guns which
made the local beauties gasp
when the pool, in frothy splashes, took in my ripped
svelte and toned body.

But today with greying hair,
pill bottles bulging, cell phone, weakening resolve
and lighter necessities only pack
I limp into the wilderness.

Only a day or two
to find nature
but most of all to prove
I'm an adventurer, a wilderness guy,
a red blooded man in every sense
(and a poet ?)
the kind of gent
who makes even
older girls and sophisticated ladies
well past their prime,
think thoughts of
cowboys, pirates, explorers,
adventurers, Marco polo
and ME !

MY GREATEST POEM EVER

the magical words
that I write

the page, stories
and books that
I leave

hopefully cause
wonder and joy

making folks
engage

in thinking and
pondering
and the reading of poetry

 reflection
about life's meaning
 and the historical past

but the
greatest poem

that We leave
written one
day at a time

is the life
that we live

SITTING BY THE TRAIL

Now more than before
I sit beside the trail
and watch
as life hurries by

I remember when
I was a part of that
constant moving stream
I cannot say that then
was better than now
for each stage of life
gives its share of hope,
joy and adventure

Back then I wanted
much
Having things was my
goal
Having things would make life
complete
Now I have those things
and wonder why I wanted them

As I sit by the trail
life seems different now
there is an aching in my bones
that only love can fill
Now I look for the little things
in each day
yesterday a rainbow
today a robin feeding its babies
tomorrow a nurse's smile

WE ARE ON THE TRAIL

a crow circles overhead
riding a thermal
dew drips from leaf and bud
between us and the shadowed mountain
rhododendron and daffodil
carpet the forest floor
a mild spring breeze
fills the senses with fragrance
as chattering chipmunks
proclaim to woodland friends
that life this moment
is God's special gift

we lift our packs
and become one with God
and pray memories of this special moment
will be with us when
as the day grows dark
we celebrate,
listing the friends
we wish were with us
but you and I
walk with God
and share some GORP

YOU ARE HERE

I keep thoughts of
your smile
in the top of my pack
and echoes of
your laughter
strewn through my things.

I watch reflections of
your eyes
in the morning dew
and smell
your perfume
in the flowers and trees.

As I walk down the trail
and
climb the mountains
I talk to you
softly
and hear you in the breeze.

I see you walking
in the shadows
asking me
to
dance with you
in
the clouds.

CAMPING

CAMPGROUND FLY

Ah, my life as a fly.
Sometimes we travel
in circles supreme.
Sometimes we land on a dog
or get stuck on a cake.

Today I'm stuck in a john
down under the seat.
The views are terrible at best,
for no one likes big butts
and little butts too,
all with something to say.

They blot out the light
and rumble and cuss
and there are hazards galore.
For some only an umbrella is
necessary, but

Bombs are the worst,
for hissing and swirling they come,
and cause such a splash.
A poor friend named Herman
is still riding a wave
that started in February
and ended in May!

CAMPGROUND MOSQUITO

As campground mosquitos
our rules are all set.
When SUV doors open with
joy and glee
we're organized,
attack plans in place
formations all set.

As pop tops go up
we zoom and we buzz
and gather donations
that put the
Red Cross to shame.

City folk give the most
all plump and fat
but seldom can smack us
as we dive by.

Then in the night
when sunburned and red
they donate some more
to the little Red Cross volunteers
always asking for more!

CAMPGROUND RAIN

Soggy campers peer from
under tarps and wet tents
as gray skies pour summer rain
on slowly filling
fire pits

White haired, over weight
old people smile through
motor home windows at
dashing mothers herding
small children to bathrooms
while fathers are walking soggy dogs

It's summer at Petoskey State Park

Board games are dusted off
coffee pots refilled and
books of fiction reread

After lunch there's shopping
and rides in the car
all the while looking to see if the sun is
coming out - it always does

we're camping at the State Park

IN THE OUTBACK

the din
and roar
of generators
hum
and groan
through the darkness
of the night
the early
dawn
finds these motor home
folks
watching carefully
the nearby woods
to
see
which animals
are
deaf.

MISSANABI STEW
(based on accidentally shaking Borax in the food)

I have this friend
who in the wild
caught some fish
made
bean salad
and accidentally
cooked them both
with a batch of
soap
and lard

we laughed
and laughed
and laughed some more
then ate
some beans
cooked with lard
and still today
I cannot say
those fish and soap
tasted any worse
than the green beans
and lard

MY BUDDY'S WASTED

empty cups
on the table
groaning
coming from the bunk
dinner
is not made
my buddy's wasted

fish
have not
been caught
fire
is not lit
aspirin bottle
spilled on the floor
my buddy's wasted

forget
late afternoon fishing
no fireside chats
tonight
my buddy's wasted

oh the evils of the
brew that makes
a man act so strange
think he'd learn
since last night
was the same

would glory be
if he had never
tasted
of the brew
that makes him
oh so wasted

(written on a rainy night in Canada)

MY OLD TENT

It's old and gray
and beginning to fray
it weighs too much
smells like burning weeds
and oh the fuss to set it up.

new tents are way cool
so easy to go up
they're bright in color
have great modern design
which make them best

yet my tent is like an old friend
with rips and tears
smells and dried bug remains
it brings back memories of
adventure and
excitement from the past

it has never let me down
so it goes with me each summer
smell, rips, tears, bugs, and all
and like a good friend
it will go with me on new adventures
down the trail

OLD REFRIGERATOR FOOD

It's gray
and
cold
It's green
and
turning brown
you see
it's very
very
old

In younger days
it tasted
good
smelled so
sweet
that even
I
know why
my friend
cannot
forgo
one last
repeat!

YUMMY TRAIL FOOD

Oatmeal
stuff horses eat
raisins
looks like dehydrated fly eggs
trail mix
nutty, seedy stuff
sardines
look and smell like our
pet fish who was dead
three days before we
found him
Ramen© Noodles
some think they look like worms
Spam©
it ain't ham and might include "parts"
chocolate bars
sticky, melted and gooey
cookies
crushed into powder
cheese sticks
what IS that oily stuff their packed in
dried soup
the peas are always hard as BB's

All eaten with a side of
lukewarm water - that tastes like plastic
and yet
when eaten under the big tree
two miles ahead
hikers will often say
"the best meal I have ever eaten!"
go figure

STIRRING THE POT

If one stirs the pot
often enough
everyone will have
something to stew about.
They may receive
their just desserts
which is not just
pie in the sky.
With old men
out on holiday
nothing is half baked.
Time allows for
slow cooking -
apples, prunes
(especially prunes)
Chefs will cook
fishermen will fish
ideas will be exchanged
discord and harmony shared.
Thanks to Budweiser
and Southern Comfort
fellowship will be displayed
in unusual quantities.
A few days away
helps reorganize the soul
find peace in solitude and
joy in simple friendships.

LOVE

love is forever

ALASKAN ODE

The mist rises off the water
and I hear the enchanted
call of the loon

A hot cup of coffee is nearby
in this land
of the last frontier

But more wondrous
than these
is I travel with ease
with a friend
whose hand I shall hold
into sunsets
yet
to come

EXPRESSIONS OF LOVE

Your smile is
etched on my soul
your face on
my heart
your laughter fills
the corridors of
my mind

Remembering
our walks
on the beach
I feel the sand
between my toes

Watching the setting sun
I think of
our embraces
hugs
gentle conversations

Forever
you walk beside me
even when
I am all alone

LOVE IS FOREVER

If tomorrow should never come
the memories of being with you
today
will bring sunshine
to light
our journey through
the heavens
to a place where we will share
the beauty of each day we spent
together
celebrating the joy of finding
each other
in this vast and endless universe
the candlelight
of our
love will forever
shine in the darkness
like a star
telling the universe
we lived
on the earth
but most of all
we found love
which like our souls
will last forever

MY "WAITING FOR YOU" SONG

I'll sing my song of love
as you fly back
into my arms

I'll dream of tender moments
to pass away the time
until I hear your voice
and see your precious smile

My mind is filled with prayer
for your safe return
when once again you will be
a part of me
and I of you

My heart will stop racing
I will again enjoy
thinking about
the wonders
of spring

REMEMBER ME

Walk in the rain
without an umbrella
Splash in puddles
barefoot or with shoes
Remember me as we did these together
years ago

Remember our simple laughs
corny puns, edgy talk
to pass away days of
joy and sadness

Remember beers, gin and tonics, and
lots of chips to make
each day special

But most of all
Remember me as a friend who cared
a brother who was there
a husband who loved his wife
and a grandpa who filled
the ice cream bowl extra full

When I am gone
Remember me with joy and gladness
for today I am playing ball with the saints
dancing with the angels

but most of all
awaiting
your coming

TO MY VALENTINE

Poets have written of love
with
"Let me count the ways"
I count the days
For each day
I have known you
I have learned to love you
more and
in a better way.

When we met
your love of life,
laughter,
beautiful smile and
quick mind
possessed my mind
and
stole my heart.

With children
on you knees
you radiated happiness
and caring joy
that
you shared
with each of us
As children grew
your beauty
and wonder for life
dazzled family and friends.

You radiate
joy and happiness
from life's miles
we have walked and shared.

I learned from you
loves grows
and grows
when it is nourished
with little kindness
practiced every day

Be my Valentine forever.

WHISPER YOUR NAME

When I am away
in the dark of the night
I whisper your name

I think of your beauty
the sparkle of your eyes
in the rain
I whisper your name

I feel your presence
see your smile in my thoughts
in the shadows
I whisper your name

I see you in fluffy clouds
asking me to sit
in the bright sun with you
I whisper your name

and wait
for you
to whisper back
to me

WHY I WRITE POEMS

I give you poems
just words
but they can fly
through the air
as hugs
when I can't be there

gifts
need to be wrapped
and carried
but
words can fly quickly
in rain and snow
early in the morning
or late at night
they zip through space

they let me open my heart
and tell you
that you are with me
at night
on the trail
where ever I go

poems will be with
you and friends
long after
I am gone
to remind you of my love

poems are just so neat
maybe my poems
will become
songs
then cowboys and rappers
will sing of
my love
for you

WHY GIVE YOUR LOVE FLOWERS

Love must be celebrated,
respected and cherished
to keep it strong
and make it grow.

Without attention
it sputters and loses its spirit
like a starving fire
on a rain soaked day.

There are many
gifts and actions that make love
grow and sparkle.
Romantic gifts seem best,
chocolate, jewelry, music,
dancing in the rain
and home made pies

Flowers are my
gift of choice.
They are special
as if God just made them for a
beautiful lover.

Their exploding colors,
fragrant smells,
intrinsic beauty.
fragile short life
tell the world that you
are in love.

They are to enjoy
in the moment
in the now.
Giving them is a special,
universal moment
for lover and loved

Life is like the flower,
beautiful,
short lived,
to be enjoyed in the moment
and celebrated
hopefully with
a kiss or two!

IT'S COLD HERE TONIGHT

It's cold
without your love
here with me
When you
are not here
I need
a sweater
Turn up the heat
Drink warm liquids
Sit in the sun
Stay in bed longer
It's no use,
I just get chilled
Return to me
Be near
and warm
my soul.

FLOWERS

I bought you flowers today
not for what you do
but or who you are

You make the bed and
wash the clothes
You do the shopping
and pay the bills
You are the sweetest person
I have ever known

You are kind and generous
You teach all day and
sing in the choir
yet smile upon
my faults

You wash the dishes and
organize the house
when I struggle you
lift my spirits and
give me hope

I bought you flowers today
for who you are
not what you do

HAPPY BIRTHDAY

How can they send a
social security check
to a pretty lady
who looks like
she is only 38?
How can the government
be so wrong?

She walks like a model
has the poise of a princess.
She charms her friends
with wit and warmth.
That she even has birthdays
is a great surprise.

I think we should
pass a law.
All those who are
as pretty as she and
stay so youthful and fun
should only have
birthdays in
leap years,
or when the cat plays a fiddle,
and a cow
jumps over the moon.

LOVE LIVES HERE

you held my hand
and walked with
me today
you complemented
the dinner
I prepared
we talked of the future
and shared
memories of fun times
you looked into my eyes
saw my needs
and comforted me
you found kind words to
calm my hurts
gave me hope
to carry on
and placed gentle kisses
upon my lips

these acts and
deeds of joy
and happiness
define and show
what love
is all about

WHEN YOU WERE THERE

When life is done
and
I look back
the days were best
when
you were there

The simple joys
became a feast
my load was
lighter
the days
brighter
when
you were there

FAMILY

"BOY"
(Aka Jack)

Angie's little brother

He came to live with us
three months ago
mom, dad, and sister
call him "Boy"
and sometimes
Jack
He doesn't seem to care
all smiles and toots
he brings lots of
Joy
to graying grandparents
aunts, sister and parents

He is like having Christmas
everyday
with sparkling eyes
sweet smile
and chubby cheeks

Boy Jack
Is like the Christmas Child
A gift which
makes the world
a magic place
filled with
peace and joy

A GRANDCHILD'S VISIT

She makes us
happy with her laughter
She delights in
stories of skunks and bears
She insists on pancakes for breakfast
Runs through the house like
a free spirit
Must always get the mail for
the neighbors
But best of all says
I love coming to your house grandpa!

ANGIE'S TREE HOUSE

Every little girl needs
a tree house
Built by grandpa
with flower boxes,
shelves to store treasures,
teddy bears, stuffed skunks,
and cool stuff to write secret letters
which disappear if a
brother or boys come around.

A place to drink Kool-aid© and
eat peanut butter sandwiches with
make believe princesses,
" callipitters"
and maybe lady bugs,
but never spiders,
bees or worms of any sort.

A tree house to
help a little girl travel
to lands and places where
puffy magic dragons and frogs live
which
if one is lucky
could turn into
a handsome prince.

A tree house Built by
grandpa
says that in his world
there is a real princess,
a special little girl
he built this house for
and lovingly
painted her name
Above the door for
"Angie"

COOKIE PRINTS

Today
a little angel
left cook prints
on our windows
doors and
coffee table

She splashed soap high
up the bathroom walls
ate handfuls of green grapes
ran nude through the house
sang silly songs
filled the house with laughter
beat the piano out of tune
picked lots of pretty flowers
and
made more cookie prints

we hope they
will not fade
too soon

but
just before
company comes
we will wash them away
with regrets
for little angels
do not
visit us
as often as
we would like

THE FAMILY REUNION

Food is always king at our family reunions.
It may have a higher ranking than
sports, grand kids achievements
or conversations about
where one has traveled
and who they have seen.

Wonderfully healthy salads come to mind
complements of the "girls"
Jen, Mary Ann, and Diane.
Freshest veggies plus unusual
special ingredients from
some far off place they visited
on elephant, lamas or wild asses.

We need to ask questions like
"hummus made from yaks what?"
"These were imported from what
third world country?"
" picked by whom ?"
Followed by brats sizzling in grease -
the exact kind my cardiologist
say to avoid
if
I want to make it to next summer...

And desserts, desserts, desserts
Rebecca finds the most chocoholic
recipes to actually die for - and from!

And Jon and Kurt's beer talk about
hops and brewing, bottle size and color

makes me wonder why
we just don't drink moon shine
and call our selves hillbillies.

Then pictures are taken.
" You never smile "
"Just once smile for your mother "
"Take one with my camera "
"Oh shoot, the flash is on!!"
"Her eyes were closed!"

Reunions often cause one to
seek premature napping
or unfortunate and unanticipated
acts of boredom -
like yawning, taking walks or
too frequent bathroom breaks.

But after all is said and done
and far too much food and drink
consumed
food comas set in.
We are leave this reunion
with smiles and good memories
talking about
recipes for next years gathering.
We all agree
WE CAN'T WAIT UNTIL NEXT YEAR'S REUNION !!

GRANDPA'S WILDERNESS CAMPING RULES

Parents have rules
Teachers have rules
The Bible has rules
Even condos have rules
But Grandpa's camping rules are different
And maybe even strange
No singing "Grandma got run over by a reindeer"
No monkey business
No funny business
No skunk business
(I'm not even sure what a business is!)

Food must be cooked over a smoky fire
Hot dogs must be slightly burned
Beans must be eaten with a
bent plastic spoon
Scary stories must be told every night
about bears and wolves chasing
kids bringing fresh baked bread
to a starving grandma who lives
in a far away woods
(don't all grandmas live in
old age homes in the city?)

I guess I can put up with these rules
Cause some of the rules I actually enjoy
Like Ice cream cones for breakfast
No combing your hair if you don't want to
Wearing the same clothes all week
Not having to stay clean

But best of all
If you don't understand the rules
Or break them accidentally
You can get extra hugs and
maybe even Extra ice cream by
pretending you are A tiny bit scared
Of this wilderness living !

I NEED A HUG

My name is Angie
I like
running through the house
jumping in the leaves
eating ice cream

pounding the piano
counting acorns
splashing in the tub

getting the mail
talking to the neighbor's dog
watching Elmo
dancing to the music

But just to make sure
I get what I
want
and what I
need
I say,
"Grandpa I need a hug!"

and like magic
Grandpa is there
and
I even get some
ice cream!

MY FIRST BIRDHOUSE

I built Christmas birdhouses for
my teacher, Aunt Jen
daddy and Grandpa Dan.

Grandpa Jer
was the most happy.
I guess he worries about
little birds
out in the cold
without a house.

He says I'm his
favorite helper
and gives me
hot chocolate
to help build
beautiful little bird houses.

I have learned a lot
about building
and grandpa and
they both are fun.

I think Grandpa's are special.
They play with you and
give you candy.
Birds just look pretty
and poop on your deck

GRANDPA IS THE BEST

He takes me camping
Lets me wear his hat
Tells me stories of
bears, lions, gators, skunks and
things that happen
on the moon
He buys me french fries for breakfast
and two scoop ice cream cones
We hot tub in the snow
and he's always ready
for pillow fights and
huge dart games
Christmas gifts are
tools and things that click and bang
He lets me help with chores
and get the mail in
rain or snow
He squirts and sprays
the car and me
Splashes in puddles
And always gives me cuddles
The pancakes we make
Are oh so delicious
and he doesn't care when I
Make a mess
He tells me stuff about
Mom an dad that I
would never hear
But best of all
He says I'm so very sweet
and a tinny bit naughty
and the best grand daughter that ever was
(hmm...any chance of some college tuition here?)

CHRISTMAS EVE

The simple joys
and many toys
the smiles of
little children

The sounds of
laughter
bells and carols
the hugs of
friends and relatives

The smells of
special foods
and fragrant Christmas Trees
the lighted homes
steeple tops
and family laughter
fills the night

Hope and love
from God
to us
through
a little child

GOLF
(memories from a golf outing with Sammie)

Today I played golf
raced through morning traffic
hurried to put on unpolished shoes
skipped sun screen
wolfed down donut with tepid coffee
forgot to tip bag boy
greeted
over excited
plaid clad seniors,
Nike© clad college boys
ogling
attractive college co-eds
swinging
designer clubs
to wait half and hour for tee time.

First drive hooked
badly into knee high
thick grass/poison ivy.
Muffled swear words into
half filled cold coffee cup

Used excuse I
was saving for major
foe pa shot on second hole
on 20 yard dribble miss.
Continued to be positive,
"The weather sure is beautiful today"!
Shouted "FOUR" to foursome 300+ yards ahead,
lost new sleeve of golf balls in first four holes,

alluded to extreme pressure at
work and home as
excuse for poor shots.

Hit beautiful 250 yard drive.

Decided golf is
game God sent
to heal troubled souls.

It just doesn't get any better than this

GRANDMOTHER'S DISHES
(garage sale time)

Faded cracked and yellow
soup bowls missing
gravy urn still shiny and bright
gold rim on plates
looking brownish red

They sit
stacked beside
old novels
and fiction
well past today's interest

Waiting to be sold
at prices discounted
many times over

The joy
and celebrations
they saw
still lingers
reflected
in the memories
of aged buyers passing by

Christmas parties
graduations
birthdays
anniversaries
They were featured at all

Piled high with
pork roast
mashed potatoes
vegetables
and cakes
of all colors and styles

Handled so lovingly
dried only by hand
placed carefully
in china cabinets so fine
out of reach of
sticky, dirty, little hands

Awaiting a future they
hope will once again be
filled with
good food and
happy families.

To hear
Silent Night
and Happy Birthday
sung out of tune -

at least one more time

JENNIFER

your logic and
cutting wit
is such a joy
your steady hand
and seasoned thought
gives rise to endless
pride
your thoughtfulness
and kind remarks
cause the heart to swell
the cards and
many little things
you do
the way you share your
love with friends
and family
makes each day a little brighter
and life's loads so much lighter

your keen and
gifted mind
your tenacity
hard work
achievements
and successes cause
much joy
we bless the day and
thank the Lord
for a daughter
such as
Jennifer

REBECCA

zany quirks
bright remarks
dancing in the aisles
notes of love
lots of hugs
funny jokes
happiness you share

trips we took
books you read
harried calls
interesting friends

the campfire chats
macaroni and cheese
camping in the Everglades

you are such a
special child
you know

songs you sing
flowers you bring
each day
we love you more

the world's
a better place
for all you give
and share

you are a
special one

a daughter
we call "Becky"

CATS

cats are cool
they do what they want
and say what they please
sleep on chairs
or place themselves
on your lap
with out ever asking

we serve them
food
and take out
their poop
we comb their fur
and scratch
their heads
and let them
sleep on our beds

cats live such
good lives
most would say
wherever
cats go when
they die is
where I hope
I shall
one day lie

LOSING WEIGHT

This morning
I thought about losing weight
just ten pounds or so
Exciting thin thoughts
raced through my mind

Could I handle the compliments ?
" damn you look good "
" so young I didn't recognize you "
" college reunion this summer? "

A reason to get new clothes

Might have to change my Facebook page

A few dance lessons
would go nicely with my new figure

A crash course in dealing
with friends' jealousy wouldn't hurt
even if it's an on line course

What about a new sport for me?
I love watching
Olympic gymnasts and
beach volley ball

And so with bathrobe flapping and
South Beach,
Weight-Watchers and
grapefruit diets
flooding my mind

I head toward the fridge

To get this thing on the road
a V8 and hard boiled egg

Opening the fridge
the light created a halo around
last nights double cheese,
deep dish
extra pepperoni pizza
~
It was delicious

SQUIRTING THE STARS

With squirt gun loaded she says,
"Let's squirt the stars, Grandpa."
That will make the night dark,
I tell the little blond girl.
Let's just squirt the moon.
We squirted low to miss the stars
and got the moon!!
It started to fade.
"What will the cow jump over"
she squealed in delight?
The man in the moon has
dealt with little squirts before!
Most squirts never get there.
It's usually as dry as a sandbox,
but if you sing "hay diddle diddle,
the cat and his fiddle
the cow jumped over the moon"
and have a little laughing dog on your lap
and are careful with grandma's plates
A spoon may go dashing by......
"How does the silverware
get out of the drawer?"
I don't know,
but getting the moon wet with squirt guns
Is a sure way to give the man living there chills.
Little blond girls with squirt guns
can be so dangerous !!!

SHOWER PATINA

men must have a dominate gene
a "patina attractor device"
for antiques
well aged artifacts
things that are rusty,
musty and dusty

not only do they seem to
enjoy flee markets
old tractors
and trains
whenever they rinse
they create
"shower patina"

in the showers and tubs that they use
the browns and the golds
that forms on the sides
growing and glowing
with each passing day
all soapy and clingy
a site to behold

now ladies
of distinction and class
find this demeanor
disgusting and crass
a health factor
for sure
to be remedied
with powerful sprays
and long handled brushes

lest mother in law
in shower
should happen to fall
and end up cussing them all !

THE 90TH BIRTHDAY

Elegance and charm
Beautiful children
Memories of well spent days
Humor and warmth
A strong and abiding faith
Peace that come from experience
The love of family and friends
Memories of many ocean sun rises
An "I can wear purple and
drink brandy whenever I want" attitude
Guidance and help for those who will listen
You have shown all of us that
"As we grow older
along with thee
We know the best is yet to be"

VALENTINE'S DAY

We share our moments and days
living in the shadows and
sunshine of love built upon years of
memories made with
beauty and trust

Each day I return to the many reasons I love you more today
than I did yesterday and yet
less than I will tomorrow

I will love more everyday
your smile,
easy, happy, playfulness,
kindness,
stellar beauty
Mona Lisa smile
and virtues many fold

But most of all I love
the mystery of you being you
I love you because you are you !
You bring to each day
all the beauty and joy of a summer's day
in each and every smile
You are the meaning of valentine
So easy to love
Thanks for being you

Love J

AGING

A SENIOR MOMENT WITH TECHNOLOGY

What's a **gigabyte**?
A nibble with false teeth?
How about **Face book©**?
Don't tell me,
a book for each part of the body.
Just the thought scares me.
Bluetooth is something I'm not sure
even my dentist wants to deal with.
I don't even want to ask what
an **iPad©** is used for.
E-mail did
we flunk out of A-B-C mail?
A **browser** sounds
like the deer in my back yard.
Laptop - desktop - handheld
suggestive.
Seniors shouldn't try any of that stuff
even if it's **user friendly**.
I like the emphasis
on **memory**,
but telling everyone how much we have is ridiculous.
Network I understand.
Being a tennis player I can always use more practice.
To **Google** something sounds obscene.
Touching all those **apps**
and playing with your **apple**...
Down loading - up loading
Where in heavens name did they
come up with these terms?
Yet technology
Is here to stay.

Young people want us
to **text** them,
Watch them on **you.tube**
and **twitter** with them
That sounds a bit strange in and of itself
Guess I'll get my wireless headphones,
grab a **Microsoft**, **Picasa** but not **spam**
and do the microwave thing.
(those little waves have to be practiced)
I'll **twitter** a bit
with an **iPhone** (or is it a me phone?)
in a **nook** or **toolbar**
or perhaps
on the **web**.
I'm starting to feel like a **tekkie**

ATHLETES BEWARE

Injuries lurk everywhere
when seniors play sports
Love the tennis but
tennis elbow waits to come courting and
planter aphasia wants to be your doubles partner
While aching Achilles tendon
rotator cuff and Mr Hamstring
All want matches......
Golf is a delight
Fresh air with friends
a few swings and then
Oh!, my back!
And what about getting the
clubs out of the car!
Ouch!
Pickle ball scores
such a strain on the brain
we aging folks are slipping
Alzheimer's - dementia can't be far behind
Shuffle board dangers are lurking with
biscuit cuts and tang contusions
Fishing sounds great
but hooks and barbs all sharp and pointy
just waiting to catch you
in inappropriate places
Bike riding is always a breeze
until vertigo spins the world
like a carousel gone wild
With injuries ready to pounce
it is hard to leave the
safety of condo and house

But onward we push
for athletes we are
Forget injuries and pain
Chiropractor
Doctors and
dentists
are awaiting our call
Round robin @ 8:00
Golf @ 11:00
Bocci @ 2:00
Pickle @ 3:00
Shuffle board @ 5:00
Happy hour @ 6:00
Dinner @ 7:00
Bridge @ 8:00
Do these seniors ever take naps?

BETH'S GOLF SHACK

When snows drifting up to my window ledge
Or I am about to go under for
MRI or surgery
I always want warm and happy thoughts
to fill my mind and take me through
At times like that
some have written about
things like the green,
green grass of home,
mother, trains or even life without pain
For me and many others
we will think of a
delightful, sunny, little building
in southern Florida
staffed by happy smiling people at
Ocean Village in
"Beth's golf Shack"
There's anticipation of great fun -
Standing in line
friendly greetings of old friends and new
It's like the U.N.
New York, Michigan ,Canada
Ohio ,Nebraska and many more
Free Advice about golf (usually not taken)
life or even history
Questions about health and family
makes one feel like it's a reunion of
long lost friends
I don't need happy pills today
I'm next in line
At Beth's Golf Shack !

DO FEET GET ENOUGH CREDIT?
(the agony of de-feet)

My name is Feet and
today I am
hurting and tired
And why shouldn't I?
I carried "team body" all day
yet everyone looks down on me
The right arm swung the racket for
two hours and then it could rest
Face smiled several times
But I had to carry it all day
Stomach may be the worst offender of everyone
It loads up on
pizza, beer and ice cream
then I have to carry the whole load
Even the skin misuses me
If it feels cool
Coats, hats, gloves and more go on
I carry all that stuff over ice and snow
And as a group
They make me do my work
In smelly dirty socks and too small shoes
If I complain about a little pain
They call me names
Like "hammer toe" or "bunion foot"
Or even "athletes foot"
Which sounds ok but really is a
Put-down that nobody wants
Sometimes the crowd up there
Misses and we even get sprinkled on
So what are we to do?
It seems we do all the work without much credit
So if you are ever hanging out with the crowd upstairs
How about just saying once
"my you have beautiful feet"

GOOD NEIGHBORS

Once or twice in a life time
people are lucky
and get wonderful neighbors
They don't build fences
between your houses
or turn you in for infractions
like noisy family parties
or grand kids pulling up flowers
Playing with worms,
beetles and "calapitters"
or double dipping on Halloween
singing at the moon from the hot tub
or borrowed tools not returned
Instead they get your mail
when you are gone
Share recipes and special foods
Turn up the heat
before you return from near or far
Alway serve up a drink or two
when times are good
or times are bad
And even though leaves are
blown into your woods
apologize with such sincerity
Some people talk about
life beyond this world
Streets of gold
Happy hours that start at noon
But my hope
is to have these neighbors
live next door
and share the soups and drinks
at least until the cows come home !

MY FIRST PICKLE BALL MATCH

What is pickle ball?
Is it like a matzo ball?
Briny thoughts race though my mind.
Pickles can be sweet or sour
To my surprise this seems
more like a whiffle thing
I see two of the gladiators smiling sweetly
Baggy shorts - muscle shirts
Two others with sour looks
Must be a dill pickle
The players swing wildly
only to see a floating yellow sphere
glide easily past their flailing paddles
Sweat soaked wanna-be athletes
Intimidating to say the least
One - five -one
Two -three-two
Are they all trying to be quarterbacks?
"Stay out of the kitchen"
Sounds good to me -
I don't like cooking anyhow
With gate ajar I enter
only a little net separates me
from their big wooden paddles
and self serving smiles
Feels like a lions cage
Fault they yell
I'm trying I respond

Watch out for the slice,
one cuts in front to poach
Mr whiffle sails past me teasingly slow
Swinging hard I not only miss the ball
But twist my self into a knot
(are we sure this isn't pretzel ball)
so far this isn't a barrel of fun
Do I quit
Or smile sweetly
Or get a sour look on my face
Now I AM in a pickle.

NOW I WANDER

Now life's work is done
career is past
friends retired,
moved, died and gone.
Children working
they now know
the way
their lives filled with
hope and expectations
Now I wander
into places
around the corners
where I didn't
have time to look
before
I'm always looking back
to days more focused
when children's
laughter filled the air.
As I wander
its neither good
nor bad
however it would be
nice to hear
a compliment or two
about a job well done

OUR STORIES

When we grow old and die
our stories remain
The history of our lives are
Obituaries in the sky
They may give hope and joy
and be fun to read
Or could be sad and depressing
And bum out all who read
We create our stories
One line at at time
Everyday writing line after line
through the way we spend our days
and live our lives
Etched in history for all to share and
read for all of time to come
Nasty, self serving, gun toting,
kind or helpful
Our book of life unfolds
in little deeds
thoughtful or thoughtless
The smiles we share
The tips we leave
The books we read
Only we, as authors,
decide what we shall be
A novel
A tragedy
Adventure
Religious instruction
Healing strategies for the afflicted
Book of philosophy
Cookbook supreme
But if I can choose
A romance it shall be
A love story
With you in love with me
And I in love with you
And ending with a kiss
And hug that never ends

SENIOR BICYCLES

Like tombstones in a cemetery
well past their prime
with leaning
faded markers
they stand In disciplined racks.
Row upon row
most rusted, dented and busted
old squeeze horns on handle bars askew
with tires so narrow
they look like an arrow.
Wide white wall tires
once in the trend
now flat and cracked
like the surface on the moon.
Fluttering ripped plastic bags cover
huge broad seats large as a Webber
baskets of wicker, plastic and canvas
2" x 4" trailer hitches
for golf carts, shopping carts and more.
Colors once bright
which use to
delight youngsters
who thrilled to their ride
now chipped and faded
grays and light browns.
These valiant
old models
squeak and groan when rode
Some with padlocks
to protect from thieves
who never come
Yet like their riders
often will give more
good years
of wonder and joy
to all who their use
want to employ
(ever wonder why seniors seldom buy new bicycles?)

THE TIP

I thought about leaving a tip today
Coffee was served hot
Waitress was friendly
But something held my money
firm within my hand
Might need it for coffee tomorrow
She is on a break - another will take it
I will tip larger next time
I don't have change
Don't want to walk back to the table
I might need a candy bar for
a sugar low this afternoon
I am in a strange town
I will never see her again
She only came to the table twice
I bet she would spend it on cigarettes or beer
Is that a dragon tattoo on her arm?
Why is she wearing a nose ring?
I know this restaurant is doing well
The pay is probably good
My friend did not tip
He must know something
Was his cup dirty?
One dollar here - one dollar there
Financial foolishness is not a virtue
If I tipped - how much?
Change looks cheap
Paper too much
I saw a man leave a gospel track
that might be nice
And so with money held tight
And head held high
I left
I saved a buck

THEY'VE ORGANIZED OLD AGE

hiking, biking
cards, games galore
swimming, ping pong
book groups, red hats
reliving Bible school
summer camp and
grade school trips combined
this AARP Group is
on the run
sun up to sun down
Biscuits and gravy
spaghetti dinners
sing-alongs
hours and days filled with
motion and action
which go on and on
and yet
go nowhere
With gray hair
and tired bodies
they pass each
saying
"See you same time tomorrow!"

THINGS ARE GETTING BLURRY

My eyes are getting bad
Starting to fade
Never see golf balls arrive on the green
Books I read are fuzzy at best
halos and circles around lights in the night
lady friends look beauteous and sculptured so fine
I know now my eyes
Not only need rest
But will not pass the simplest of test
But what shall I read
in case improvement is lost -
If today's reading is my last?
Love letters are memorized deep in my heart
Perhaps the Bible might be best with a second coming
To take us away from all maladies and pests
Books from the past seem quaint - out of date
Homer, Socrates ,Plato and especially Descartes
Reading cookbooks seem to make one fat
Self-help books seem egotistical and self serving
Large print seems best
But lined up in aisles with gray hairs
Selection is so depressing
Children's books are nice
But smiling while reading
Gives one strange and unhealthy glances
So reader beware
It's time to give grandpa
his chair
headphones
music boxes
iPods and
Jam boxes

A BOOK

I look
upon a book
and often see
stories told of
maidens, men
or philosophy

of horses
dogs
mysteries and
things yet
untold

I love my books for
they will be
with me and
keep me company
when
I shall walk into
my last night
and death
shall be my mate

they will give me
hope and
joy
for books like
beer, wine
and good friends are
easy company

CONDO RULES

CLOSE THE GARAGE DOORS
NO CLOTHES LINES
EACH UNIT WILL BE PAINTED THE SAME COLOR
NO FLAGS OUT FRONT
QUIET PLEASE
NO PETS ALLOWED
NO ROLLER BLADING
SKATE BOARDING NEVER
LAWNS CUT TO 1"
NO KITE FLYING ALLOWED
DO NOT PARK TRAILERS OUT FRONT
NO CHILDREN UNDER 50 PLEASE
TURN RADIOS DOWN
NO LATE NIGHT PARTIES
NO FLOWER POTS ON DECKS
DO NOT WASH CARS IN DRIVEWAYS
NO OVERNIGHT GUESTS
DO NOT FEED THE BIRDS
ALL CARS PARKED IN THE GARAGE AT NIGHT
NO CAR ON STREET AFTER 10:00 PM
NO SOLICITING
NO COOKIE SALES - THIS MEANS GIRLS SCOUTS TOO
NO TRICK OR TREATING
NO GARAGE SALES
NO RUNNING ON THE SIDEWALKS
NO CHRISTMAS LIGHTS OUT FRONT
(YOU MAY PUT OUT WHITE 6" CANDLE
IN CENTER OF LIVING ROOM WINDOW ONLY)
APPROVED CONDO GREETING
"ANOTHER WONDERFUL IN PARADISE"

I'M GRAY &
STILL WORKING

Each morning I leave early
friends my age
still in bed
retired heading to classrooms to
sit reading with grand kids
watching snakes at the zoo
drinking two pots of coffee
scarfing up late morning tee times.

My colleagues talk
at water coolers about
wings, football, tailgating and
beer parties I'm far to old to enjoy
but I'm still working.

The money is good
and piling up
love the recognition
and oh such pride
a watch for forty year would be.

Pain in my arms, legs
back and chest
been to the Doc
so young she could be
my grandchild.

So when my time
at the office is finally done
my friends all grey
and living in Florida
proudly I'll say
my life was my work
my work was my life

I've never scheduled
a tee time during the week.
What is the weather
like in Florida?
What in the heck is Pickle Ball?

Was it worth it?

MR. STIFF-N-ACHY

A new friend lives at our house.
He slipped in
when we weren't looking.
He's not loud or noisy,
but he's such a pain.

He's at our back
when we pick up things,
climb the stairs,
or make the bed.

He's right there
every morning
when we get out of bed.
He's even in the shower
when we drop the soap.

But now
he has a name
"Mr. Stiff-n-achy"
and
I think I like him more.

He says he is going to live here
for lots of years to come.

At least
he is easier to complain about
than the cats
or my wife.

MY GLASSES

They are on
my head
until I'm dead.
They go with me
in rain
and snow.

They are
by my bed
each night
when I lay me
down to sleep.

They sparkle
when they are clean.
Some say
they make
me look intelligent.

They help me see
and hold
my nose in place.

I love
my glasses
for when I die
and turn to dust
my glasses
will be
all that is
left of me.

OLD MEN

They walk with a limp
these slow moving old gimps.
They're in bed by nine
and they groan
when forced from their beds
these crusty old men.

One look says
they're half dead with
bellies protruding
hair all grey
and falling out.

Wives correct them
when to the
bottle they go and
they gasp
when they walk.

So why do
we care
about these old bags
of hot air?

The interest is
there for
surely we'll share
the pains
and the aches
that we'll never repair

if not tomorrow
the next day
for sure.

RETIRED

I walk mostly alone
and much more slowly
to find beauty
that was here
all the time

I sense
the purpose of
the seasons and
see shadows from
the future
flickering
across my way

I watch
sunrises
with awe
and feel holiness
gently
entering my existence
as I
become one
with God

FIRST DAY OF SCHOOL – RETIRED TEACHER

Like sounds of distance thunder
rolling off buildings
I hear echoes
of children's voices
noisy in the halls.

I feel my sore throat
getting dryer
answering questions
about lockers, lunch and recess

I hear the PA system
announcing after school meetings
the smell of strong coffee in the lounge
and this stiff collared shirt wears
heavy on my neck
the bell is ringing to start another class

My eyes slowly open
its just my alarm
it is the first day for kids
it is 8:00 AM
the sun high in the sky

Today I will enjoy first hour's class
in my living room chair
with my dog,
coffee and newspaper

and many wonderful memories

THE BEST IS YET TO COME
(making life meaningful as a senior)

If we are lucky we
age gracefully.
We move slowly away from
the many walls, barriers and confines
we spent our working years
building and refining.

Efforts to provide security and
happiness through
success, prestige, accumulation of wealth,
mortgages, financial goals and plans.

Only to discover
they never were that important.
Friends move and die.
Money is lost along with
the best of intentions.

ON THE ROAD

A CANADIAN SUNRISE
9-21-99

golden rays
creep through pines
on dainty little feet,
yellow poplar
become a blaze
with flames,
as morning
sun
enters the
world
without a sound.

Birds awaken
and sound
the entrance of
a new day,
golden light
spreads its
warmth through the
woods.

Another beautiful
sunrise

MY PRAYER

Touch my soul with
Your spirit
fill my heart with
Your joy.

Open my eyes
to see
the needs in the world.

Fill my journey here
on earth with
caring and healing.

Make my life a
testimony of
Your love.

Walk with me here today
help me comfort
those in need.

Let my life be
meaningful
as I
serve.

IT'S RAINING IN PRINCE RUPERT

the rain is
falling
in
Prince Rupert

it falls
and
falls in
little patters on
the camper
like
the crackle
of
frying bacon

its raining in
Prince Rupert

is it
raining
where you are?

THE ALASKA I REMEMBER

a never ending
ribbon of
tar, asphalt
cement and gravel
winding and crawling
over mountains
plunging down
through
narrow passes
dated gas stations
1920's hotels
log cabins
broken down houses
up and up
over majestic mountains
so high
snow rides in swirls beside me
and water rushes past
like horses racing
down a canyon
lupine carpet the way
as I feel
the tired groan
of the old Dodge
climbing higher
and higher

THE ALASKAN WAY

they passed
like large boxes
on a conveyer belt
some small
some medium
but most large
expensive
motor homes
driven
by
bald or
white haired
fat men
a string of
never ending
white
refrigerators
looking
for moose
and
bear

THE BROOK

This noisy brook
is like a child
running, jumping, splashing
and dancing
hurrying to become
a big strong river
to carry
on the business
of the world.

Little streams
like children
lose their
sparkle and innocence and
become
powerful and strong

As sunlight filters
through the trees
reflecting on silver water
I sit in silence
watching the little stream
thinking that
I would rather
hear a brook laughing
see children dancing
than watch a
strong river flowing
or listen to
a lawyers song

THE CITY CAMP
(at Traverse City State Campground)

    the throbbing roar
    Of the Harleys
    ate the morning's
    silence
    too quickly
    to enjoy any
    lingering
    dreams

    faint night
    memories of
    coolers being
    sacked
    by hungry coons
    disappear
    in the calls
    of gulls
    scrapping
    over refuse
    left by last nights
    sleeping campers

THIS RIVER, PLATTE
5/25/00

This water
pure and cold
flows past in
silvery splendor
harbors ducks
and fish,
turtles and
snails.

Like the
people I meet
it passes
through my thoughts
in swirls and eddies
and carries
the things
nature drops and
cannot hold.

Like the people
I meet
it soon is out of
sight and
on its way
for others
soon to greet.

WINTER PRAYER

God bathe my soul
in the light of
your holiness.

Refresh my spirit
with joy
from above.

Lift my burdens
and let me breath in
the wonder of
your glory.

God give me faith
and hope to
share your majesty
and salvation.

Let me walk each day
with you
beside
me.

GAMES CAN HEAR THE RAIN

They hear
the pitter patter
of the
rain
and see
the drops
streaking window panes

It is then
the games get
bold
and quickly unfold as
they come from under beds
and push open
seldom used cupboards

They squiggle from behind
chests of drawers
jump up on tables
or just sprawl on the
floor

Their pieces and dice
spread out in attack
causing players
to yell
and occasionally show
strife

But when the sun
shows through the windows
and falls onto the floor
They head for
cupboards
slide under the beds
waiting for
rain
fog
or even some snow

REFLECTIONS ON TWO BEAUTIFUL DAYS IN GODERICH

Those days went by way too fast
Good friends make life delicious
Rambling walks are under rated
New places sharpen our senses
Slowing down life's pace - wonderful

Life with My love -
joy unspeakable
Only time for opening thoughts
Better than a relative reunion
So much joy

Let's schedule more time next year
Living among hurting people can bring focus
Life greatest gift is to be a giver
Living in the now fully is a worthy goal

Friends let their friends win at golf
Goderich may deserve another visit
Our time there sets the table
For a winter feast of ideas in Florida

Hotel$$, food$$, golf$$, gas travel$$
Friendship with Each of you - priceless

NEW CAR MEETS THE TRADE-IN

They sit side by side
briefly
on the new car lot
flags flying.

Smiling, plaid jacketed
sales staff
greeting customers
like oldest of friends.

Only a short
glance of introduction
between the two.

The new
shiny and bright
brisling with electronic
gadgets and gizmos
eager to take on tomorrow.

The old
tired and bent
smelling of French fries,
baby vomit,
and spilled coffee,
tires dirty and wore,
paint faded and splotchy,
dents from Frisbee, baseball
and hail.

The new
proud
of the high price it demands.

The old
embarrassed
by the pittance offered in return.

After all the trips to the store
school, hospital and even the time
we pulled mother in law
out of the ditch,

would just $50 more
be asking too much?

REFLECTIONS ON A PADDLE DOWN THE BUFFALO RIVER IN ARKANSAS
(A spring trip)

Time flies when you're with good friends
A River's beauty enters your soul, shapes your spirit, forever fills your dreams
Vultures float on thermals, selecting vulnerable, unsuspecting paddlers
Around the next bend lies adventure
Why does this have to end?

Those who catch fish walk with their chest out proudly,
Look here, look there, fish, big fish, just below the canoe
Swimming, swimming in the crystal clear water
Why can't my buddies catch them?

Extra sticky, lumpy oatmeal, those poor horses
Eggs and spam frying, I'm in heaven
Will we run short of food ? My buddy has Paydays !
Why did I pack so many items I will never use?

I must come back here soon
The full moon on the river is a picture gift one never forgets
One hour on the river was well worth the many miles to get here
Water's so clear, is this a mirage?
Water dripping off a paddle, a quiet melody that calms the troubled soul
Stone knockers, tree frogs, wandering hoot owls - nature's symphony
Wet feet, dirty shorts, sunburn, sleeping on the gravel - price of admission

Wilderness paddlers have solutions to all of life's problems
Slowing down life is such joy,
pick up your paddle....just float.....live in the now
The serenading beauty of the quiet stretches suggests a holy place
Ancient peoples, early American paddlers loved this river
It's a place to find your self, reset priorities -
Do I really need to work until I'm 75?
I would love to take the naysayers on just a one hour paddle

THE SPIRIT OF BEAVER ISLE

tourists of all
sizes,
occupations and
temperaments
try to discover the
"Spirit of Beaver Isle"

Is it in the wooded wild?
the crashing waves upon the shores?
the inhabitants warm and friendly smiles?
the long gone history of an ancient king
with wives a plenty?
maybe its in the winter winds that howl across the ice
or pale blue skies and balmy breeze of summer?

for me the Spirit of the Isle is
the magical wonder
which keeps folks coming back
for discovery,
intrigue,
or to be refreshed,
and wanting more of the
mind expanding beauty
the island has to offer

THE DEER HUNTERS

Having spent mega dollars on gear
they walk stealthily
faces painted black
brightly clad in orange
spritzed with doe urine or fox piss
pockets bulging
with ammo
two way radios and cell phones
protruding
from techno pockets
backpacks stuffed with snacks
(prepared by tired wives)
they carry rifles sized to kill elephants

these deer hunters
who loaded
corn and veggies into
four wheel drive trucks
to lure in hungry deer
are about to
brag about bagging
a big one

YOUNG DEER HUNTER
(dedicated to Craig Hoebeke 2001)

Sleep wanders in and out.
It's the night before the hunt.
No dreams of girls
or Ms Brown in third hour.

I have the gun and shells,
jerky's all packed,
compass is in place.
Uncle Tim is snoring loudly.

Should I shoot a doe
or wait for the trophy buck?
Should I sit up in the tree or
traipse in the woods?

The corn is out,
my flashlight is ready.
Two pair of socks or one?
I want to be in the woods at 5:00
the old men say 6:00.

Where is the sleep I need
for the adventure
of going
into the woods -
where the bucks are huge
and cougars, fox and bear
will watch my
every move?

OUR CAR'S INTERIORS

(tell who we are)
With bobble heads,
hanging dice,
and ten year old ash trays
half filled with coins
some cars are like
riding in a Family Dollar Store.
Religious cars
have crosses hanging
on mirrors,
St. Christopher praying
on the dash,
and baby Jesus riding
shotgun in the back window.
Pet lover's cars
smell like dogs,
have Kibble and Bits
on the floor,
chewed throw toys under the seats
and half filled water dishes
which splash on your shoes.
Fast food lovers
have cars that
smell like French fries
are filled with McDonald bags
and cups with
every available door pocket
filled with
catchup, mustard and
leaking mayonnaise containers.
New parent's cars
are fitted with car seats,
twisted mirrors

to watch every little smile and toot
hanging toys to entertain,
blankets, books, and diapers,
and the ubiquitous "Baby on Board" sign.
OCD cars are unbelievably neat,
pine tree air fresheners hanging,
leather so clean it squeaks,
map stored neatly in the back seat pocket,
windows sparkle brightly
(no finger prints on these)
even the keys shine
The eclectic hoarders is my favorite of all.
You can find coupons for
any thing on the floor,
old condiment packets on the seats,
church bulletins from Christmas 2010
library books,
numerous cassettes with
tape hanging out,
toys, empty cans, clothes,
perhaps
your missing sweat shirt
from the family reunion
three years ago.
It labors climbing hills
with its cargo in tow,
but it's home on the go -
even if there is an over riding
feeling that you are traveling
in a dumpster on wheels!

REFLECTIONS

LITTLE LIGHTS

I love little lights
on Christmas trees
candles in windows
flashlights in pup tents
soft lights in church
and twinkling stars.
Sitting close to
small camp fires
reading books under blankets
dim lights in halls.
Little lights
with glow so small
say come be with me
my spirit is yours
to nourish and hold.

I find God in little lights
It seems He
needs me to
love and share the
warmth in
even the littlest of
lights.

ME CLIMBING TO HEAVEN

I laughed
a lot
drank a few
and caused
a stir or two

I thought
and read
and fantasized
of days gone by
and things to come

some thought
I was a pain
others thought
I made them think

those who called
me friend
helped get me
through this life

when I am gone
if I could hear
a story
of how
days were
better
because old Jer
was still there

I might just
return

MORNING COFFEE

It is hot
It is brown
I love it's taste and
of all the food I know
it gives the greatest comfort

It greets me every day
with smells so fine
It is there
when days are hot
and surely there
when days are cold

It's been with me
watching children grow
and on the trail
after funerals it is there
even to church
it sometimes goes

it is drunk with friends
relatives
in-laws and outlaws

I've drunk it from plastic
paper, tin and glass
beer mugs
wine glasses
and sippy cups

it's best
when I'm alone
for it helps
me think of you
with
cat on lap
slippers and housecoat

MY JOURNAL

this book
is a part of me
and I
a part of it

it tells me
where I've been
and
what I have done

I tell it stuff
and treat it rough
but it
still goes with me

I tell it secrets and
it hides for me
who I've kissed
and other naughty
stuff

it holds
my poems
big ideas, bad ideas
philosophy
and other
heady stuff

and yet it goes with me
for when
I quit
and tell it nothing
it is no more
a part of me

it is the end
of
a hopefully
well told
story

REFLECTIONS ON A SCHOOL YEAR

They came through the doors in
September
sat through the snows of
January and February
considered the birds and the bees in
April and May

I taught what I knew
Did I feel their fears, pains and
ambitions?
I knew what I taught
Did they see my fears, frustrations, and
valiant attempts?
I started class on time
Did they share their hearts and minds?

I smiled and greeted them
Did I give them what they needed?
I demanded their best
Did they meet my limited tests?
I finished the year
Did they hear what I said?

Summer is here
sixty days of vacation
Time to recharge

THE SCHOOL PARKING LOT

It is raining
It is Monday
The flag
hangs limp
and droops.

Teachers open
SUV doors
spread newspapers over
heads and
run for
the school.

Big yellow busses
arrive with
lights flashing,
belching smoke and
rocking with the
noise and excitement
of children
pent up for
the entire weekend.

School is beginning
The pledge will
be said

I wish I was still
in bed !

WILLIE'S LAST DAY OF SCHOOL

Willie
was very poor
just up from Mississippi
sat near the back
his eyes seldom moved
his mouth never

Did Willie have dreams
hopes,
ambitions to be great
or successful?

Had he ever loved someone?
Did someone love him?
What was his favorite song?
Did he ever have a pet?
Had he ever seen Lake Michigan?
Did he have a brother?

The talkative, aggressive students
seemed to take all my time

Willie left today

My chance to know Willie is
gone
forever

6-1981
Ottawa High School

THE THINGS I BUY

the things I buy
I think
I need
I've told myself
and planned ahead
so when I get
just what I want
how happy I will be.

so now I have
the things I want
and knew I
needed,
but
as they age
and old they grow
I see them less
and less
and wonder
just
what it was that
made me think they were
the things I wanted
and thought I needed

THIS MOMENT IS MINE

this moment is mine
I'm in it
I feel it
I know how long it will last
I see it's shape
I know when it started
I hear it
I smell it
my coffee shares it with me
I record it
so I can take it with me

A POEM ABOUT YOU

Everyone wants
to read a poem about themselves
which highlight their
beauty and intelligence,
fun loving personality,
wonderful things they have done,
and please don't forget the places
they have been all over the world,
college degrees
as well as volunteered
prayed with the sick
Comforted the dying and given
Money to the poor.

But poems are about
how the writer feels about the person.
This is a definite problem
you now can easily see
for authors are like God.
Controlling the pen and writing the words
and each idea they select to write about.
Poems about people are usually just a
record of the past.
Each and every person prepares
their own poems each day they live
by all they say and do.

But just in case an author writes by other creed
I suggest you buy them a coffee
or lunch whenever possible.
(good poets like waterfront restaurants, or so I'm told)

I'M RUNNING

I'm running
across the room
to get to grandma
down the halls
to get to class
through the aisles
to get the best sales
running
running
running
down the highway
to get to work
through the winter
to get to summer
through life's work
to get to retirement

but today I will walk
to hear grandma's
cricket story
to watch
the birds playing
to see
the flowers blooming
to smell
the cookies baking
to get
a hug from grandpa

runners often leave the present
too fast
to get to the future

IT'S NOT ABOUT ME

Why wine when it's cloudy
We need less sun screen those days
Some folks are stuck
In the snow and the cold

Why talk only about me
Other lives are as exciting
and meaningful
I can't learn new facts from me
I know all about me

Gifts from me are more fun
than gifts to me
If I took me to dinner
It would be boring
I'd chose the same thing every time

It's not about me
It's about u

U are different and exciting
U bring me fresh ideas
U See the world from a different perspective
U are a peep hole Into the
meaning of the Universe for me
I love u
I wish u the best

SPIRITUAL WALKING

I've walked spiritually.

It was often on a sunny morning
on the Appalachian
Usually in nature

A quiet time
Often walking alone
standing looking backward
and forward facing life

Listening to waterfalls,
watching rainbows, birds and insects
in joyfully symphony
declare the glory of God

Feeling nature surround me
in warmth
saying,
"I'm a part of God plan"

Crickets sounding like baby angels
The wind whispering
Holy, Holy, Holy

A warm mist on my face
telling me I am alive
living in this marvelous
creation

I've also been with spirit people
who help guide us into spiritually
Like Ms Sue-nap
And sages of old

They say words and blessings
which like sounds in silence
help take us out
of darkness
Into the joy and light of happiness

I have found that
walking spiritually is a choice,
a place where
we often meet God

A place to walk slowly
be still and
bare foot if possible

A place we all can go
for spirituality
is inside ourselves

In all of creation
It is the miracle of life

THE DO IT NOW LIST

don't die with your song inside you
don't pass away with your
poems unwritten

letters of encouragement must be mailed
notes to comfort the grieving sent
our gifts and tithes must be given
before the final count is taken

the gracious compliment and
good words must be said before
our voice is but a whisper.
deeds of charity, helping the poor,
repairing their homes, preventing war
must be done soon
or father time will take away our
best intentions

to light our candles
we must get them out of the closet
each small light can unite with others to
brighten a sometimes dark and dreary world

sharing this is part of my
do it now list

THE FLAVOR OF WORDS

Words can fill our minds
with the nuances and flavors
of a world filled with joyful
delights and mental adventures
or one a bit crude and hard to swallow.

"I just threw the salad together "
could have been
"Aren't fresh vegetables great?"
"I just pulled it out of the closet"
Instead of
"I just love the color light blue"

Words chosen to uplift
and show refinement
are such a pleasure to be around.
Words are condiments of the mind
"flavors of refinement "

I just cleaned the "crap" out of my garage
sounds hard when compared with
"relocating all the stuff I
thought I needed yesterday
To a place where it hopefully will be used".
"it's going to be hotter than hell today"
"it's a great beach day today"

I think I would rather spend my day with
thoughts of the latter waffling though my mind.
Words influence our thoughts and
those around us in so many ways.
"He is so stupid"
Or
"everyone struggles at times"
So you choose
"Damn it's going to be a rough day"
Or
"bring it on I can handle anything "

What flavor will you choose?

THE PEOPLE THAT WE MEET

The people that we meet
are peep holes
into the soul
of
the universe

The way we see them
and treat them
open
or closes
passage ways into
the origins of
our beginnings

Together they form
a mosaic
which tells a story
of life's
origin
A history of the universe

People are the cells
that make up
the living hope
love and
All that many call
God

We are all part of its
magic wonder
Together we find
purpose and joy
and reason for
life itself

PHILOSOPHY

BROTHERS

one black
one white
our American journey
so different

advantages and opportunities
for some
racism
scaring hopes and ambitions
weakening and defeating spirits
for others

will we ever both share
the promise and
wonders God
has so blessed
in this beautiful land?

even those of privilege
when in leadership
let callused greed be their guide
and propose
harmful deeds
and twisted progress

will we who walk
such different
journeys
ever share a
bond of hope
and love to secure the future?

glimmers of hope
arise now and again
when in pain
we sort out the past
and agree to help each other
into the fragile future

CHOICES MEN MAKE

Our choice......
To destroy nature or live with it's wonders

A motorcycle's roar on woodland trail
breaks the afternoons solitude
The ATV and skidoo fractures
the peace and tranquility
Of watching a loon feed its babies
Or
A canoe and kayak ease among the lily pads
And see a dragon fly land upon a floating stick

Shotguns blast the cloud filled fluffy air
bringing down gulls, crows and ravens
Or
Enjoying their calls more than the smell of gun power

Shooting prairie dogs for random fun
Wasting little creatures who are
guarding families from hawks and coyotes
Or
Using a camera
to record their family life and marvel
how God lives in all of life She created

Snowmobilers roar through silent snow filled
woods and fields
chasing deer, rabbits, fox and squirrels
Fun for us.....panic for them

We all make choices
For me I choose the quiet sports
and often find that those engaged in such
have a deeper understanding
of the spiritual
for the lack of motors roaring and guns killing
gives time to meditate about the soul

DIFFERENT OPINIONS

Are we still
friends ?
For strongly held
thoughts
plans
politics
and even
worship styles
differ so
that when discussed
cause such pain
make me wish
that I were with
"the bright and best "
who are just like me
and yet when I'm
alone I think of you
and want your company
so
"how's the weather there" ?
on this we can
agree
Its cool and wet here
Coffee tomorrow?

LIFE

milk
bicycles
first kisses
introspection
finding direction
education
choices
opportunities
options
transcending my constrictions
need to wander
new experiences
old friends
new friends
childhood myths
general relativity
quantum mechanics
donuts
coffeecake
love
ashes

LIVING IN THE NOW

caught between
yesterday and tomorrow
like peanut butter and jelly
on a sandwich
we try to live fully in today
but feel the aches
and pains of yesterday
the anxiety
of what is coming tomorrow

hoping the doubts
cares and fears of today
will not appear in new shapes
and forms in the future

living in the now is our quest
fully, exciting, productive
being satisfied with hope
and simple joys
giving to those in need
getting rid of greed

we start by being calm
asking questions
taking suggestions from lives
well lived
taking small steps of kindness
and gratitude
helping the fallen
protecting the weak

like an infant we grow fast in wisdom
and knowledge
the now begins to feel comfortable
affordable, achievable, predictable
like the song of a bird
or a baby's first words

we feel the now
as we become more
and more
a part of the whole

OUR PLACE IN THE UNIVERSE

People are peep holes
Into the soul
Of the universe

The way we treat people
Clouds or brightens
Our view and understanding
Of God

Each person is one important
Small piece of this unique
And marvelous creation

Discrimination,
fear,
Not sharing the worlds resources,
Thinking we are selected for heaven
They for hell,
Makes us live in darkness

The way to truth and salvation
Is sharing the
suffering and hurt
Of
all people

OWNING STUFF

When I was young
and times were tough
I'd seldom share
I loved my things
and giving stuff was very rough
for having things
and owning stuff
was such a joy
It made me feel such sweet success
the more I had
the more I stored
my basement overflowing

But now I'm old
and wiser some
and storing stuff
and owning things
is really quite a chore
Taking care of things
is just a bore
and moving things
is worst of all

Now I find sharing things
and giving stuff
has become my joy
This thing I give you now
is gone from me
and yet it's memory
gives me joy
would you like
some more stuff?

TRUE HEROES

Some people spend millions
work countless hours
to have their names
put on museums,
opera houses
and even churches.

The love of many
is to see their names
on arenas,
gardens
or even theater lights.

Often these favors are bought
with cleaver deals
made with politicians
who need the dough
to keep them on the go.

But like the fire fighters,
police and
rescue folk
of NYC
my hope
would be to leave
my final footprints in
the rubble of life
helping the suffering,
needy
and scared

"we found his footprints
going in when the world
was running out"

WHY DO WE HATE?

Why it is there
in the souls of men?
I know not.
It stalks us
walks with us
and makes
us say
and feel
such terrible things,
after which we
feel guilt
and shame which
follows in close
pursuit.

I think we help
it grow, this hate and strife
by being small
and fearing love.

For when we
say
"I love you"
the hate is
gone
and we begin
to heal again.

WAR

scares birds
mothers hate it
young people fight it
nations fear it
religion exacerbates it
songs glorify it
politicians exploit it
military plan it
citizens die in it
blood banks store for it
wives cry an grieve during it
soldiers are maimed in it
angels collect souls during it
gun factory's make money from it
the environment is destroyed from it
veterans remember it
children suffer from it
pacifists try to stop it
evil thrives during it
God allows it
poets write about it

love prevents it